P9-ARA-943

Inniskillin

ANATOMY OF A WINERY

THE ART OF WINE AT INNISKILLIN

DONALD J.P. ZIRALDO

FOREWORD BY
HUGH JOHNSON

INTRODUCTION BY
KARL KAISER AND DONALD ZIRALDO

DESIGNED AND ILLUSTRATED BY
SAM TURTON

KEY PORTER BOOKS

Dedicated to my Mom, Irma, and Dad, Fiorello.

My father died in 1964. I was 14 years old. In 1971, at my graduation from the University of
Guelph, my mother presented me with my father's ring. The ring is solid gold from the
McIntyre Mine in Timmins, Ontario, where he worked underground for 23 years. In 1974,
three years later, I opened the winery. I have never removed the ring which I wear to this day.
As if by destiny, the ring depicts clusters of grapes, vines and tendrils.

All author royalties from the sale of this book will be donated to the Cool Climate Oenology & Viticulture Institute at Brock University, Canada

Special thanks to Canadian Pacific Hotels for the photography from the book "Great Canadian Cuisine" by Anita Stewart.

Photography for front cover: Yuri Dojc

Technical Support: David Sheppard, Assistant Winemaker, Inniskillin Wines Inc.
Project Support: Deborah Pratt, Director of Public Relations, Inniskillin Wines Inc.
Photography:
Kevin Argue, pages 33, 50, 53(R)
Cosmo Condina, page 42
Dieter Hessel, pages 15, 44, 45, 46, back cover inset
Yuri Dojc, front and back cover, pages 12, 52(L), 56
Steven Elphick, pages 5, 41
James O'Mara, front cover, pages 3, 10, 13, 17, 25, 29, 39, 40, 41, 43, 48, 55
Sara Matthews, page 14, 55
Scott McIntyre, pages 50, 52(R), 53(L)
Mark Shapiro, page 49(R)
John Sherlock, pages 50(T-R), 52 (L), 53(B-L)
Niagara Parks Commission, page 16
Sam Turton, page 54(B)

Engraving: Yves Baril, page 13

Copyright © 1995, 2000 Donald J.P. Ziraldo
All rights reserved. No part of this work covered by the copyrights hereon may be reproduced or used in any form or by any means – graphic, electronic, or mechanical,
including photocopying, recording, taping or information storage and retrieval systems – without the prior written permission of the publisher, or,
in case of photocopying or other reprographic copying, a licence from the Canadian Copyright Licensing Agency.

Canadian Cataloguing in Publication Data
Main entry under title:
Anatomy of a Winery
Rev. ed.
ISBN 1–55263–141–9
1. Inniskillin Wines Inc. 2. Wine and winemaking – Ontario – Niagara-on-the-Lake. 3. Wineries – Ontario – Niagara-on-the-Lake. I. Title.
TP559.C3Z57 2000 663'.2'00971338 C00-930225-5

Key Porter Books Limited
70 The Esplanade
Toronto, Ontario
Canada M5E 1R2

www.keyporter.com

Printed and bound in Canada by Friesens
00 01 02 03 04 5 4 3 2 1

www.inniskillin.com

FOREWORD

Each of the world's classic wine regions has a distinctive identity of place. It can be as obvious as the Médoc, a long tongue of gravel and sand lapped by the Atlantic on one side and a broad river estuary on the other, or as subtle as the Côte d'Or, which on first sight seems interchangeable with a score of other hillsides in eastern France. However, when you get to know them well, their terroir, the sum of climate, soil and terrain that stamps their personality, becomes almost tangible; their style of wine its somehow inevitable product.

The vineyards of the Niagara Peninsula come into the "obvious" category. How could any territory be more clearly defined by nature than this lake-locked, escarpment-sheltered stretch of country? Its success as a fruit garden has long been well established. But until the 1970s it waited for its discoverers to realize it as wine country; the modern Canadian equivalent of the eager monks who created Burgundy (but with poverty, chastity and obedience optional).

Then suddenly it happened. Old fears and prejudices about the kinds of vines that could survive in Canada were tossed aside. The formidable know-how that has been accumulating in new wine districts round the world provided answers to problems that had seemed insuperable. The 1980s saw Ontario take its place at the high table of the world's cool climate wine regions. The 1990s saw it finesse its style, identify its most privileged sites and build its reputation beyond regional interest into the mainstream of the world's acknowledged fine wines.

Nobody will deny that in all this the Inniskillin winery has been the ice-breaker.

Yet the creative dedication of Donald Ziraldo reaches far beyond his own winery. As Chairman of the Vintners Quality Alliance he is shaping the ambitions of Canada towards truly distinctive estate wines; the only route to international respect and trust.

And by the imaginative educational weapon of Inniskillin's self-guided winery tour he is teaching the new generation of Canadians to understand and appreciate the wines their country can make. This book is the logical, portable extension of the self-guided tour. It compresses, graphically and ingeniously, all the essentials of wine-knowledge into an evening's study.

I salute Donald Ziraldo, his partner, Karl Kaiser, and the staff at Inniskillin for another initiative that will demystify wine and bring it more friends. And I salute that ever-growing band of friends of wine and life.

HUGH JOHNSON

Author, **World Atlas of Wine, Pocket Encyclopedia of Wine &** *others; host of T.V. series* **Vintage: A History of Wine.**

"It was those Cistercians who started it all. They tasted the soil. They found the medium for expressing what they had discovered about the land they were working. And of course, they created a masterpiece for all time, one of the great masterpieces of the western world . . . the Cote d'Or.

"Well, there are new masterpieces in the making, and I visited one this morning by helicopter. The other side of the lake. The Niagara Region. Nothing can be more thrilling than finding, being shown, a new wine region where these possibilities are being taken seriously."

Hugh Johnson; *excerpt from speech presented at the Granite Club, Toronto.*

Above, from left: *Donald Ziraldo, Hugh Johnson and Karl Kaiser at Inniskillin*

INTRODUCTION

I decided to reissue this book to commemorate our 25th Anniversary (1975–2000) and the Millennium. I have revised the book slightly and added more specific information about Icewine, our involvement in the Okanagan, and CCOVI, the Cool Climate Oenology and Viticulture Institute which is named Inniskillin Hall.

The Inniskillin winery exists because we believe that the making of wine is an art and that the experience of tasting good wine is one of life's greatest pleasures.

Like all art forms, winemaking is deeply connected to the mastery of inspiration and creativity. Every grape variety is unique and is affected differently by the soil of each vineyard and the weather of every season. A winemaker's knowledge and intuition lead him through a labyrinth of choices, from grape variety and style of fermentation to oak variety and barrel aging. At every tasting, each wine unveils something unique. Capturing the essential characteristics of each wine at its moment of perfection is the art of winemaking. It is what we take pride in at Inniskillin.

The initial idea for this book grew out of the popularity of the self-guided tour on-site at the Inniskillin winery. We had discovered the concept of a self-guided tour at Sterling Vineyards in California's Napa Valley. We drew on this inspiration to devise our own tour, cutting viewing windows into the old and new buildings, so we could provide comfortable sightlines to all the viewable aspects of the winery and vineyards. Commentary, illustrations and photography set up at each viewing station explain the process of winemaking step-by-step.

The response was phenomenal and many Inniskillin visitors asked for written information about their experience on the tour. In answer to these many requests and because we felt a real need for more information on our wine-growing region, the first edition of *Anatomy of a Winery* was written and published. Since the original idea, it has grown and developed into an educational tool to provide additional knowledge about cool climate viticulture.

We have focused, in this book, on cool climate viticulture. Therefore, we did not include a chapter on our Napa Valley venture where we, Inniskillin Napa Vineyards, are producing wines under the Terra label. Carneros, where the Chardonnay grapes are grown for Terra, is considered a cool climate region relative to northern Napa and Sonoma.

We are very proud of our many achievements at Inniskillin, such as our being awarded the coveted Grand Prix d'Honneur at Vinexpo in Bordeaux, France for our 1989 Icewine. The Icewine continues to gain international awards and worldwide recognition. A truly Canadian success story.

Inniskillin has prided itself on being a leader in the industry and to this end has made a commitment to support Brock University's Cool Climate Oenology and Viticulture Institute (CCOVI). In recognition of our commitment the facility is named Inniskillin Hall. It will support future generations of winemakers and viticulturists with advanced research and education as we invest in the future of high quality Canadian wine.

The evolution of wines in Canada has been nothing short of phenomenal. Red wine development has accelerated rapidly, through clonal selection and canopy management and I see Pinot Noir finding a very quality-focused niche in Niagara, while Merlot is the focus in the Okanagan.

As well, we are very proud to share in the success and evolution of Canada as one of the rising stars in the quiet revolution of New World wines. We thank you sincerely for the support and enthusiasm which has inspired us to achieve the successes thus afforded Inniskillin and the opportunity to create this book in celebration of our twenty-fifth anniversary and the Millennium.

1975–2000.   ENJOY!

DONALD J.P. ZIRALDO
CO-FOUNDER

KARL KAISER
CO-FOUNDER

COOL CLIMATE VITICULTURE

Canada's Niagara Peninsula in Ontario and the Okanagan Valley in British Columbia are considered cool climate viticulture regions, as are Burgundy, Germany, Oregon and New Zealand. Temperatures during the fruit-ripening phase are moderate and consistent. These regions are ideally suited for the growing of Chardonnay, Pinot Noir and Riesling. Wines from cooler climates are characteristically higher in acids and highly aromatic. These high acids result in wines, particularly white wines, with longer natural aging potential. Winemakers believe that cool climates produce lighter, fruitier wines whereas hotter regions produce less fruity, heavier wines.

Wine was grown in the cool climate viticulture regions of Burgundy and Germany as early as the first century. The first vineyards were established by the Romans, although it is believed that the Gauls had domesticated some wild vines for winemaking long before the Romans arrived.

It is also thought that the Pinot Noir grape is an indigenous variety of Burgundy. The resistance to winter frost is a major characteristic of the grape. Quality Pinot Noir is best achieved under cool climate conditions such as the Niagara Peninsula, while in warmer climates it loses its elegance and finesse. A slow, even maturing process of the grape clusters on the vine seems to be a prerequisite for the manufacture of delicate aromas and freshness. Micro-climatic differences influence the behaviour of Pinot Noir and the broad variation that can be found from vintage to vintage is an expression of that sensitivity. A good example of this is Pinot Noir in California where the cultivar best expresses these characteristics in the cooler Carneros region of Napa and Sonoma.

Chardonnay, on the other hand, is much more adaptable across a wide range of climatic conditions and can exhibit vastly different personalities. In warm climates, such as Australia, Chardonnay tends to exhibit ripe, dense fruit flavours such as pineapple and mango paired with low acidity. Chardonnays from cool climates are characterized by their delicacy, finesse and firm acidity with subtle flavours of apple and grapefruit.

In general, cooler continental climates such as the Niagara Peninsula and the Okanagan Valley are subject to greater extremes – that is, hotter summers and cooler winters – than those of the warmer regions of Europe and California, resulting in considerable variability between seasons and vintages. Vintage charts from cool climate regions, such as Burgundy, show much more variability than do most vintage charts from hot climates such as Italy and Australia.

Cold winter temperatures are a significant limiting factor in viticulture. Winter injury can be common and if the temperature falls below -20 degrees Celsius (°C), bud damage can occur. In North America, commercial viticulture is traditionally confined to southern regions such as California or water-moderated regions such as Long Island and Niagara. Continental viticultural areas are not only exposed to lower mid-winter temperatures, but are also subject to greater fluctuations in temperature during the maturation of the grape cluster (veraison to harvest). This results in a greater temperature range and consequently more variable vintages.

Northern latitudes, generally associated with cool climate viticulture, have shorter growing seasons. As a result, the rate at which grapes accumulate sugar and lose acid is slower than in more southern regions, so they develop truly interesting flavour profiles unique to the area.

Latitude is also important as an indicator of climatic suitability. Latitude and altitude affect

Odour-active compounds are easily detected by the nose and are recognized as the familiar smell of grape (primary) aroma. An example of these aromatic esters and aldehydes would be terpinol in Gewürztraminer which produces a "spicy" odour.

There are several ways to measure the wine-growing potential of a region. The most common is growing degree days. These are measured as the sum of the average daily temperatures over 10° C, below which there is little, if any, physiological activity in the vines, from April 1st to October 31st. In terms of growing degree days, cool climate viticulture areas are mostly regions that are below 1450 growing degree days. More importantly, it is the temperatures to which the grapes are exposed from veraison through harvest that create classic cool climate wines.

The following chart shows the median growing degree days in the major cool climate viticulture regions.

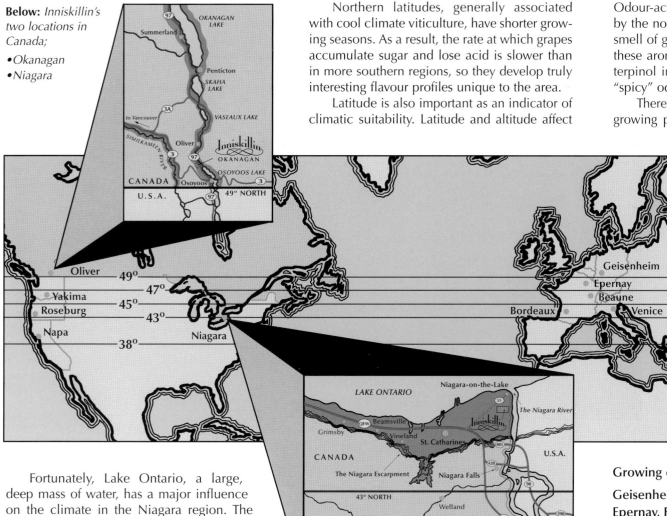

Below: *Inniskillin's two locations in Canada;*
- *Okanagan*
- *Niagara*

Fortunately, Lake Ontario, a large, deep mass of water, has a major influence on the climate in the Niagara region. The lake absorbs and stores vast amounts of heat which it releases whenever the surrounding air and land are cooler than the lake. This continuous airflow over the surface of the land moderates winter temperatures and also reduces the risk of spring frost and early fall frosts. By providing this frost protection, Lake Ontario enables the region to experience temperatures capable of maturing fruit late into the year, much longer than other areas nearby.

the amount and length of sunlight during the day and the relative coolness of night-time temperatures. In cool climate viticultural areas, low solar exposure during fruit maturation produces high levels of odour-active compounds.

Growing degree days measured in Celsius:

Geisenheim, Germany	1050
Epernay, France (Champagne)	1050
Hawk's Bay, New Zealand	1200
Roseburg, Oregon	1250
Geneva, Switzerland	1250
Beaune, France (Burgundy)	1315
Niagara, Canada (Ontario)	1426
Oliver, Canada (British Columbia)	1423
Yakima, Washington	1426
Napa, California	1450
Healdsburg, Sonoma, California	1755

The total amount of heat in growing degree days above 10° C, necessary for Riesling, Chardonnay and Pinot Noir varieties, should be between 1050 and 1450. The large range for temperature accumulation is part of the reason for the variability in wine character notes (aroma, bouquet and balance) between different regions of the world.

The hours of sunshine and the temperature in a region play an important role in the growth potential of the vine. These two influences are interrelated but should not be confused. In cooler climates, temperature rather than sunshine becomes the limiting factor in determining the potential for growth. In warmer climates, temperatures are already adequate and it is the number of sunshine hours that will ultimately govern maturity and quality.

As a perennial plant, grapevines have developed mechanisms to ensure survival during seasons of unfavourable weather. However, to ensure long-term consistent production and to maintain the required quality of fruit in cooler climates, man becomes part of the survival mechanism through proper vineyard management.

Many factors are important in the grapevine's ability to manage cold endurance. The grower must understand the nature of vine maturation, dormancy, canopy management, training systems, rootstocks, water and soil management, nutrient requirements and clonal selection to ensure that the vine is properly prepared for the temperature extremes it must survive.

Clones are selected from a large population of grapevines. They exhibit superior characteristics and have two functions: to achieve specific

and unique quality and consistent productivity. Clonal selection has played a large role in the development of cultivars specific to cool climate growing conditions. It enables the grower to select definite characteristics which, though not always immediately evident, may have a significant impact on the quality of the finished wine.

Besides the climate, a wine region's soil structure and texture greatly determines the heat retention and water-holding capacity of the soil. This greatly influences the vine's performance and thus the soil's structure is considered to be of even greater importance than its chemical composition. Climate may be the determining factor in deciding where to plant grapes and which grape varieties to plant, for example, Pinot Noir in Niagara versus Merlot in the Okanagan Valley. The terroir, however, will continue to be debated as the great contributor to the art of wine.

One of the most famous wines produced in cool climate viticulture areas is Icewine (see pages 49–51). Icewine can be grown only in cool climate conditions and owes much of its greatness to the very high level of acidity in the wine. This acidity is necessary to sustain the great equilibrium between it and the tremendous concentration of sugar in the grapes and results in a beautifully balanced wine which has great finish on the palate.

The most important factor in Icewine production is low temperature (-8 or -10° C) during harvesting and crushing which increases the extract, fullness and aroma in the wine. The resulting high acidity, inherent in cool viticultural areas, is necessary to obtain the typical character of Icewines and is even more important than the sugar level of the grapes at harvest. Icewine is a high-risk wine, as yields are very low – often as little as 5 percent (fluid extract versus total crop weight at harvest). The risk is even higher in Germany, where prolonged cold temperatures are less regular.

THE NORTHEAST

The Northeast Wine Route is possibly the longest wine route in the world, extending from Long Island to Pelee Island. In addition to Ontario and New York, there are wine regions throughout the northeast, such as Ohio, Pennsylvania, Michigan, Vermont, and Quebec.

This region is considered an area of cool climate viticulture, and each district has its own distinctive microclimate. Glaciers from the Ice Age created a unique terrain of prominent geographical features that define the outstanding wines of Ontario and New York.

Canada's Vintners Quality Alliance (VQA) recognizes three designated viticultural areas:

Pelee Island
Lake Erie North Shore
The Niagara Peninsula

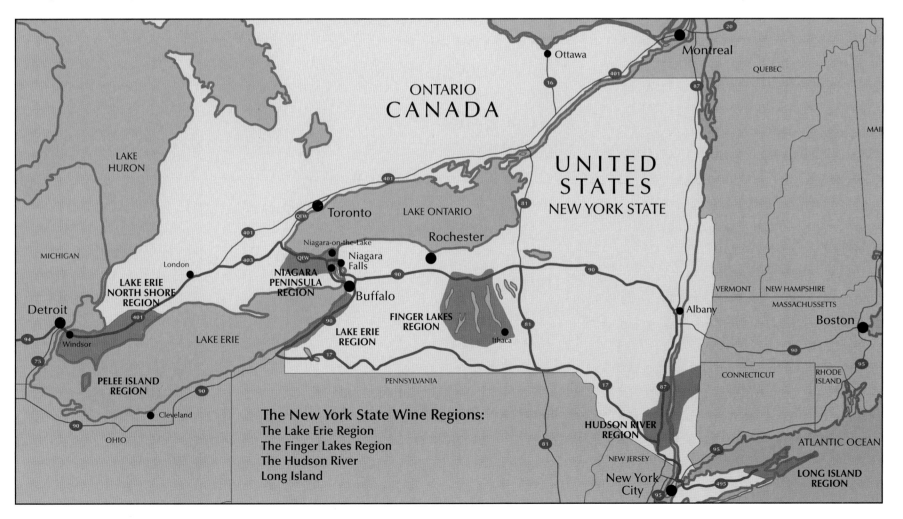

The New York State Wine Regions:
The Lake Erie Region
The Finger Lakes Region
The Hudson River
Long Island

ANATOMY OF A WINERY

In *Webster's Ninth New Collegiate Dictionary,* the description of the word "anatomy" reads: "anatomy/Gk anatome, fr. anatemnein to dissect,: a separating or dividing into parts for detailed examination or analysis."

I chose the title *Anatomy Of A Winery* to reflect the self guided tour. The twenty stations ("stations of the vine") of our on-site tour separate into parts the various aspects of grape growing and winemaking for a more detailed examination or analysis. The book follows both the vinification path and the path that our visitors take as they walk through the winery.

Anatomy also implies an "opening up," to look inside at how things work. Both the tour and the book are designed to do just that – open up the doors and walls to let you walk inside the world of wine.

It is amazing that, out of all the agricultural and industrial applications, no other single entity is more visited than a winery. This is because winemaking is more than an agricultural and industrial application of technology. It is an art form.

Below: *Station 11.* **PRESSING**

SELF GUIDED TOUR
Station Titles

1. HISTORY OF INNISKILLIN
2. THE CLIMATE
3. SOIL AND GEOGRAPHY
4. VINTNERS QUALITY ALLIANCE – VQA
5. VITICULTURE
6. GRAPE VARIETIES
7. HARVESTING
8. COOPERAGE • The Art of Barrel Making
9. HISTORY OF THE CORK
10. DE-STEMMING/CRUSHING
11. PRESSING
12. FERMENTATION
13. RED WINES
14. WHITE WINES
15. TANK CELLAR
16. BARREL AGING • The Influence of Oak in Wine
17. BOTTLING LINE
18. BRAE BURN VINEYARD
19. ICEWINE
20. FRANK LLOYD WRIGHT

WINE BOUTIQUE

HISTORY OF INNISKILLIN

On July 31, 1975, Inniskillin Wines incorporated and its founders Karl J. Kaiser and myself, Donald J.P. Ziraldo, were granted the first winery licence in Ontario, Canada, since 1929.

Established in Niagara-on-the-Lake and taking its name from the early history of the area, Inniskillin was founded upon and dedicated to the principle of producing and bottling outstanding wines from select wine grapes grown in the Niagara Peninsula.

In 1971, I received my degree in Agriculture from the University of Guelph, after which I operated a family nursery specializing in fruit trees and grapevines. Karl, a native of Austria, had moved to Canada after meeting and marrying his Canadian wife, Silvia. He had a degree in Chemistry from Brock University and had begun experimenting with home winemaking.

One fateful day, Karl bought some French hybrid grapevines from me at the nursery and, some time afterward, we shared a bottle of Karl's home-made wine. After a lot of dreaming and talking, we decided to apply for a wine licence. None had been issued since 1929.

The late General George Kitching, Chairman, Liquor Control Board of Ontario, shared our vision of "a premium estate winery producing varietal wines from grapes grown in the Niagara Peninsula," and with his assistance, Inniskillin was born. We owe a debt of gratitude to this very insightful individual.

The first Inniskillin winery was housed in an old packing shed at the family nursery, two kilometres (km) from our current location.

The name Inniskillin is Irish and is derived from the famous Irish regiment, the Inniskilling Fusiliers. Colonel Cooper, a member of this regiment, served in North America in the War of 1812. On completion of his military service, he was granted Crown land which he named the Inniskillin Farm.

We were on our way.

As we grew, we needed more space, and in 1978, we relocated to our present site, The Brae Burn Estate.

In building the new winery at Brae Burn we wanted to combine our experience with those of both the Old and New World wine regions to create an estate winery that would harmonize

architecturally with the natural and historic surroundings and create a Canadian character. The winery was designed by Raphaele Belvedere, a local architect, to allow our technological needs to blend with the historic environment of our site. It is adjacent to the existing Inniskillin vineyards, planted in 1974 by myself, and now known as the Seeger vineyard. The result, we believe, is a fine marriage of purpose, function and aesthetics.

The Brae Burn Barn

The historic Brae Burn Barn, constructed in the mid-1920s, houses the winery boutique. The main floor consists of the retail wine boutique and tour centre, while the upper level loft, maintained in its original open-beamed structure, features a training centre and demonstration kitchen for guest chefs, and a gallery.

The barn and several others in the area were constructed in a similar style and are thought to be designed or influenced by the famous architect Frank Lloyd Wright, who designed the Larkin Building in Buffalo, New York.

Architects have admired the functional simplicity, integrity and craftsmanship of the barn. The word "barn" was originally created from the old English words *bere*, meaning barley and *ern* meaning a place for the laying up of any sort of grain, hay or straw. At Inniskillin we have adapted the meaning of barn as the laying down of fine wines.

The Millennium Project

In response to the great interest in agri-tourism and our focus on the culinary arts, we are looking to the future by planning a major expansion/renovation.

Into the next millennium we will be increasing our vineyard acreage and expanding our barrel aging cellars. With our continued interest in cuisine, we will also be constructing a Wine Education Centre focusing on the culinary arts.

In keeping with the existing facilities, the architecture will, of course, maintain its "organic" theme – "to make the building belong to the ground" – to celebrate the style of Frank Lloyd Wright.

Inniskillin has commissioned renowned architect Bruno Freschi to undertake this project.

Right: *The Brae Burn Barn and Wine Boutique.*

Below: *Engraving by Yves Baril, master engraver, who also engraved the Canadian Parliamentary Library on the Canadian $20 bill.*

THE CLIMATE – Niagara Peninsula

As we discussed earlier, Niagara is considered a cool climate viticultural region, as are Burgundy, Germany, Oregon and New Zealand. These regions are ideally suited for the growing of Chardonnay, Pinot Noir and Riesling. Wines from cooler climates are characteristically higher in acids and highly aromatic. These acids result in wines that have longer natural aging potential. Malo-lactic fermentation, a natural microbial process, is used to reduce total acidity and add balance and finesse to the wines.

The Niagara Peninsula is located on the 43rd latitude, placing it in the same latitude as Northern California though more southerly than Burgundy, which is on the 47th latitude. With an average annual heat summation of 1426 growing degree days Celsius (see page 7) the Niagara Peninsula falls into the category of cool climate.

Climatically, the Niagara Region is similar in many respects to Burgundy. Both are far from maritime influence and instead are influenced by a continental climate. The annual rainfall of both is approximately 700 to 800 mm and each can experience unpredictable September and October rains. The flowering in both regions generally occurs between the 10th and the 18th of June, and although Burgundy experiences slightly more frost-free days than Niagara, we enjoy longer periods of daylight during July. Throughout the growing season, both Burgundy and Niagara enjoy long periods of daylight.

The special attribute of Niagara is the moderating effect of Lake Ontario (illustrated in Chart A, lower left) combined with the topographical influence of the Niagara Escarpment (see photo, opposite page). Together, the lake effect on temperature and unique airflow accentuated by the escarpment creates a unique microclimate that allows for the growing of Vitis vinifera. This particular growing region is approximately 50 km long and varies from 10 km in width to less than 1 km. The region can be further subdivided into even smaller climatic zones as we have illustrated in Chart A.

If one uses a comparison based upon growing degree days (the summation of all degrees accumulated over 10° C during the potential growing season from April 1st to October 31st), the Niagara Peninsula compares favourably with some of the finest cool grape-growing areas, such as Burgundy or Region 1 in California (as defined by University of California, Davis, Climate Regions).

The most critical aspect of the growth cycle, as shown in Chart B, is that growth between bloom (June 10–18) and harvest

(September–October) has approximately the same ripening period as other wine regions throughout the world, 100–112 days.

You will note that in Niagara this critical period is warmer than regions such as Alsace and Champagne. The graph in Chart B also illustrates that the cold winter temperatures in Niagara, which allow for the production of Icewine in December and January, generally will not affect the vines because they are in their dormant state during the fruit harvest and processing.

Opposite page top: *Sunset over Lake Ontario.*

Opposite page bottom: *Great Lakes region.*

Left: *Niagara Escarpment at Queenston as seen from the Brae Burn Estate.*

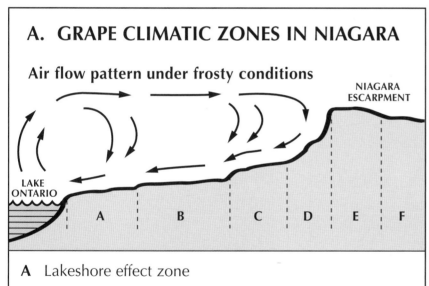

A. GRAPE CLIMATIC ZONES IN NIAGARA

Air flow pattern under frosty conditions

NIAGARA ESCARPMENT

LAKE ONTARIO

A   B   C   D   E   F

A   Lakeshore effect zone

B   Level plain between escarpment and lake

C   Base of escarpment slope plus steep slope east of St. Catharines

D   Steep north-facing escarpment slopes

E   Slopes above the escarpment

F   Flat and rolling land south of the escarpment

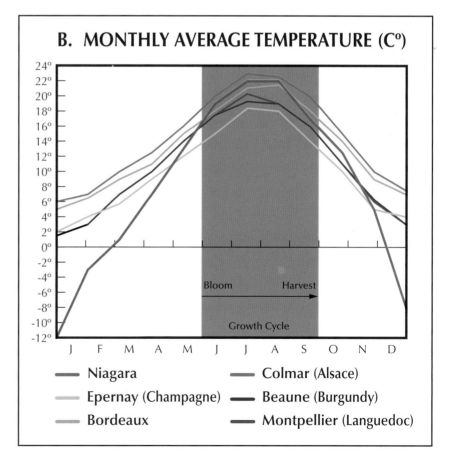

B. MONTHLY AVERAGE TEMPERATURE (C°)

Bloom   Harvest

Growth Cycle

J F M A M J J A S O N D

— Niagara   — Colmar (Alsace)

— Epernay (Champagne)   — Beaune (Burgundy)

— Bordeaux   — Montpellier (Languedoc)

SOIL AND GEOGRAPHY – Niagara

Soil is a very critical element in viticulture. What follows is a description of the physiology and geology of the Niagara Peninsula, both of which ultimately affect the growing of grapes.

The Niagara Peninsula (see map below) is a distinct geological region situated in Southern Ontario, at 43°N in latitude. It is bound on the north by Lake Ontario, on the south by the shores of Lake Erie, and on the east by the Niagara River.

The backbone of the peninsula is the Niagara Escarpment, a cuesta (ridge) 30 to 50 metres high. This escarpment extends along the entire Niagara Peninsula and influences the soil and creates microclimates. North of the escarpment is a flat plain, the result of deposits of lacustrine clays, sands and gravel whose original source was the bottom of the old Lake Iroquois (see illustration opposite page). Lake Iroquois was a single lake that existed before the last Ice

Age which caused the formation of the existing five Great Lakes. In some places the soil is modified by river valley alluvium, mostly sand and gravel. It is only in this area below the escarpment, and on the first bench, where the confluence of the escarpment and the lake favour the growing of premium grapes.

The types of rock found in the bedrock of the escarpment are siliceous sandstones, ferruginous sandstones, limestones and dolomites of Devonian age. Since the escarpment was at one time the shoreline of Lake Iroquois, the deposited soil is composed of many different types (clay, clay-loam, loam, sand, etc.) and changes frequently. The soils are generally deep and obtain a considerable quantity of mineral material from the different types of bedrock. All these rock types contribute material to the soils and ultimately influence the nutrition of the vineyards.

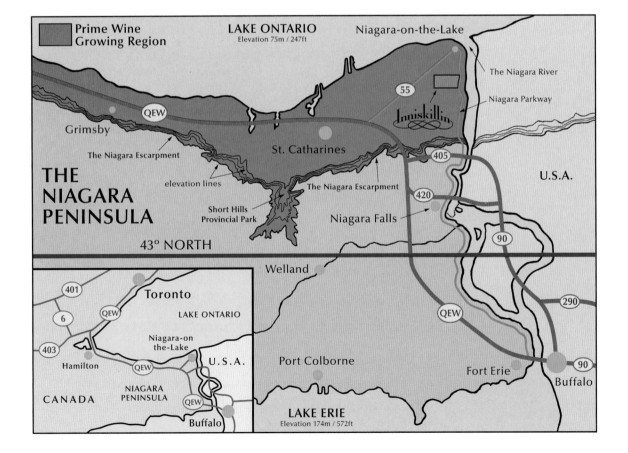

ANATOMY OF THE NIAGARA ESCARPMENT AT THE CANADIAN HORSESHOE FALLS

52 m
170 ft

55 m
180 ft

HARD DOLOMITE

SOFT SHALE

LIMESTONE

SHALE

SANDSTONE

SHALE

SANDSTONE

Niagara Falls

One of the two critical elements that are responsible for the mesoclimate which allows us to grow Vitis vinifera grapes in Niagara is the Niagara Escarpment. About 12,000 years ago Niagara Falls actually cascaded over the face of the Niagara Escarpment at Queenston, and has since moved downstream through the gorge approximately 11 km to its present location at the Horseshoe Falls at Niagara Falls. The tumbling waters, as seen in the illustration above, cut away the softer layers of sandstone and shale below the hard top layer of dolomite limestone which over the years has created the 11 km Niagara Gorge (see photos above right).

Opposite page right: *Canadian Horseshoe Falls dropping over the Niagara Escarpment.*

Left: *Face of the Niagara Escarpment with exposed bedrock.*

Below: *Queenston-Lewiston Bridge crossing the Niagara River and the Niagara Gorge at the Escarpment. See photo page 15.*

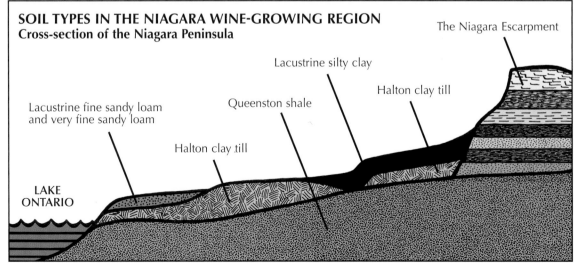

SOIL TYPES IN THE NIAGARA WINE-GROWING REGION
Cross-section of the Niagara Peninsula

The Niagara Escarpment

Lacustrine silty clay

Halton clay till

Queenston shale

Lacustrine fine sandy loam and very fine sandy loam

Halton clay till

LAKE ONTARIO

VINTNERS QUALITY ALLIANCE – VQA

The Vintners Quality Alliance – VQA – is an Appellation of Origin system by which consumers can identify wines of Canada based on the origin of the grapes from which they are produced.

With the VQA system, Canada joins other leading wine-producing countries in developing a body of regulations and setting high standards for its finest wines. In 1935, for example, France introduced its *Appellation d'Origine Contrôlée* system that remains in place today. Italy introduced its *Denominazione d'Origine Controlata* designation in 1963. Germany's *Qualitatswein mit Predicat* system was finalized in 1971, and the US system in 1978.

In Ontario the VQA officially started in 1988. The Ontario VQA then requested that British Columbia undertake a similar system, which it did in 1990. Each region maintains several unique rules and regulations that are specific to it, just as Burgundy and Bordeaux do. All wine-growing regions in France function under the French Appellation of Origin system, governed by the *Institute National Des Appellations D'Origine* (INAO).

Experience has shown that certain vineyard areas, because of their favoured soils, exposure and microclimate, produce the best wines year after year. By designating the appellations of origin on the label, vintners provide the consumer with information about the origin of the grapes, particularly the terroir in which they are grown. As in the centuries-old wine regions of Burgundy and Chianti, refinements to the existing regulations within the VQA are continually being made.

There are two distinct wine-growing regions in Canada – the provinces of Ontario and British Columbia.

The VQA recognizes within Ontario three Designated Viticultural Areas (DVA): Niagara Peninsula, Pelee Island and Lake Erie North Shore. In British Columbia, the VQA recognizes four DVA: the Okanagan Valley, the Similkameen Valley, the Fraser Valley and Vancouver Island.

The VQA is a legislated wine authority.

A stringent code of regulations governs the right of vintners to use these highly specific geographic designations on their labels. Only Vitis vinifera varieties such as Chardonnay, Pinot Noir

DESIGNATED VITICULTURAL AREAS
IN ONTARIO
Niagara Peninsula
Pelee Island
Lake Erie North Shore

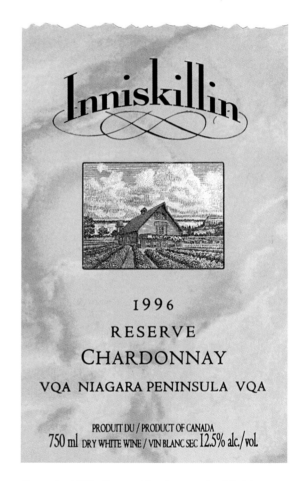

Above: *Inniskillin Reserve Chardonnay wine label for 100% Niagara Peninsula grown grapes.*

and Riesling can be used. The wine must be produced from 100 percent Ontario-grown grapes. For varietals, 85 percent of the wine must be made from the variety named on the label and must exhibit the predominant character of that variety. If a vintner wishes to designate the vineyard from which the wine was made, the site must be within a recognized viticultural area and 100 percent of the grapes must come from that vineyard. Wines described as estate bottled must be made from 100 percent grapes owned or controlled by the winery in a viticultural area. Minimum sugar levels have been set for vineyard designated and estate-bottled wines, as well as dessert and Icewine.

Wines are evaluated by an independent panel of experts. Only those wines which meet or exceed the production and appellation standards are awarded VQA status and are entitled to display the VQA medallion.

VQA Canada was formed in July 1995.

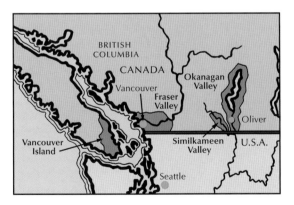

DESIGNATED VITICULTURAL AREAS
IN BRITISH COLUMBIA

Okanagan Valley
Similkameen Valley
Fraser Valley
Vancouver Island

HOW TO READ AN INNISKILLIN WINE LABEL

The Winery

Appellation of Origin:
Designated
Viticultural Area

Vintage

Grape Variety

Vineyard Designation

Alcohol by Volume

Capacity

VITICULTURE

All grapevines originated as wild vines. Grape culture is believed to have begun in the region between and to the south of the Caspian and Black seas, where grapes were first domesticated. Asia Minor, as this region is known, is home to the Vitis vinifera, the species from which all cultivated grape varieties were derived before the discovery of North America. In the Bible, in the Book of Genesis (IX, 20), Noah was said to enjoy growing grapes and making wine. Several centuries before Christ, vines were carried to Greece, then to Rome. It was the Romans who were generally responsible for spreading vines throughout Europe.

All vines are in the botanical family Vitaceae (see chart). Grapevines are of the genera, Vitis (from Latin *viere*, meaning to twist), vines which climb by tendrils. Vitis is then separated into two sub-genera, one of which is Euvitis. The principal species of Euvitis is Vitis vinifera (meaning wine-bearing), the Old World species that produces over 90 percent of the world's grapes. Some of these species are recognized as the Classic

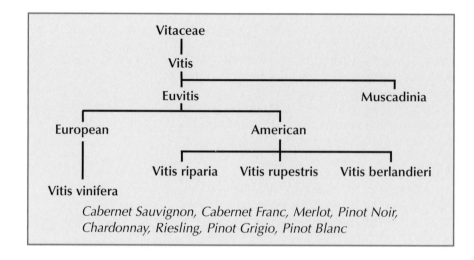

Vitaceae

Vitis

Euvitis — Muscadinia

European — American

Vitis vinifera

Vitis riparia — Vitis rupestris — Vitis berlandieri

Cabernet Sauvignon, Cabernet Franc, Merlot, Pinot Noir, Chardonnay, Riesling, Pinot Grigio, Pinot Blanc

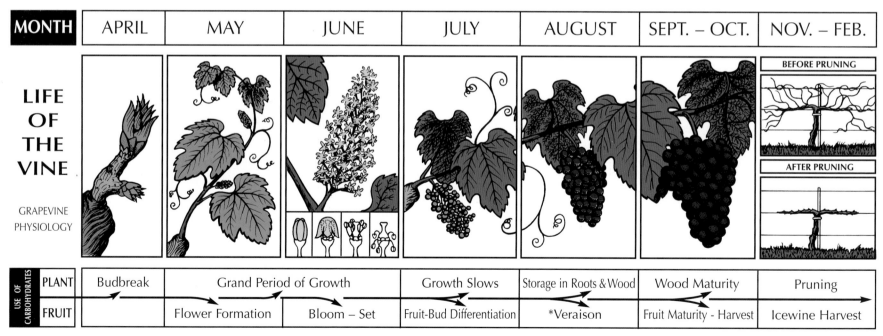

MONTH	APRIL	MAY	JUNE	JULY	AUGUST	SEPT. – OCT.	NOV. – FEB.
LIFE OF THE VINE (GRAPEVINE PHYSIOLOGY)							BEFORE PRUNING / AFTER PRUNING

USE OF CARBOHYDRATES							
PLANT	Budbreak	Grand Period of Growth		Growth Slows	Storage in Roots & Wood	Wood Maturity	Pruning
FRUIT		Flower Formation	Bloom – Set	Fruit-Bud Differentiation	*Veraison	Fruit Maturity - Harvest	Icewine Harvest

*Veraison: The point during the grape maturation process at which, simultaneously, the unripe grapes begin to change colour and their sugar content begins to increase.

varieties, such as Cabernet Sauvignon, Cabernet Franc, Merlot, Pinot Noir, Chardonnay, Riesling, Sauvignon Blanc and others. Grapevines were spread from region to region by mankind. This is often mentioned in the Bible. It is apparent that the grape has been a food to mankind from the earliest of times.

Grapevines in North America, such as Vitis riparia and Vitis rupestris, found primarily in eastern US and Canada, and Vitis berlandieri, found in southwestern US and Texas, are also species of Euvitis. These species are inherently resistant to phyloxera vasatrix (see story to the right) (Daclylosphaera vitifoliae), the root louse, which is also native to North America. Phyloxera is largely controlled by the use of these species as rootstocks. To prevent phyloxera infection, which is basically restricted to the soil, the Vitis vinifera species are grafted onto resistant rootstocks from the above species.

Vitis vinifera vines first appeared in North America via the Spaniards in Mexico and then were planted in the Baja region of California in the late 1600s and in the late 1700s arrived at the Mission in San Diego. In Canada, wild vines, probably Vitis riparia, were discovered by Jacques Cartier and later by Jesuit missionaries in the 1600s along the St Lawrence River. Vitis vinifera was introduced into Canada in the 1940s and came into commercial production in the 1970s.

An Interesting Story: When vines were first brought back to Europe from America by an adventuresome explorer in the mid 1800s, the phyloxera was a "stowaway" and soon infected the non-resistant Vitis vinifera. That epidemic almost wiped out the European wine industry in the 1860s. In Europe it was discovered that by planting the resistant rootstocks and grafting the Vitis vinifera on top of the phyloxera resistant rootstock it would not be attacked by the soil-borne phyloxera. This practice is now common throughout the viticultural world.

Grape blossoms in June.

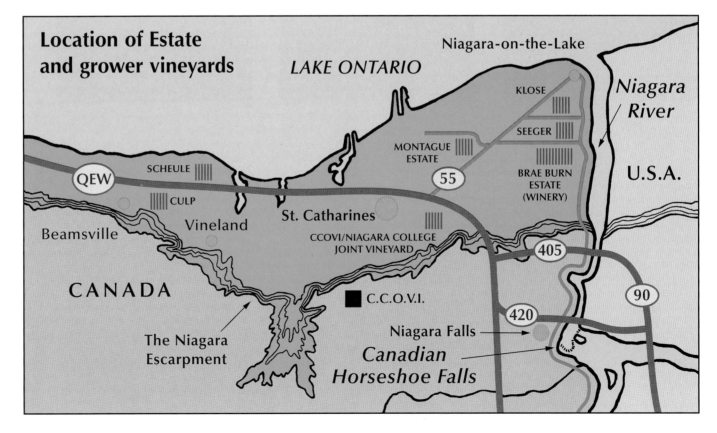

GRAPE VARIETIES

White

CHARDONNAY
(Shar'-doe-nay)

PINOT GRIGIO
(Pee'-no Gree-geo)

RIESLING
(Reese-ling)

PINOT BLANC
(Pee'-no Blawn)

The reigning "King" of Burgundy is responsible for some of the most famous, and undoubtedly finest, dry white wines in the world. Prized for its stellar quality, Chardonnay is now widely planted throughout the wine regions of the world.

HARVEST	– mid-season ripening: late September to early October
SOILS	– preference for clay-limestone soils
CLIMATE	– performs best in cool climates
YIELDS	– low: (40–60 hl/ha)*

Pinot Grigio is the Italian name for the French variety Pinot Gris. In Germany it is known as Rulander. It provides a super-rich, usually dry wine that can be partnered with food without the distraction of too much aroma. It has participated in a renewal of enthusiasm in the New World. Medium-bodied, enduring flavours on the palate, aromas of fresh, ripe pears, with a hint of spice.

HARVEST	– mid-season ripening: late September to early October
SOILS	– deep, rich, loamy or volcanic soils, or sandy, stony soils
CLIMATE	– cool climates preferred
YIELDS	– moderate: (40–60 hl/ha)

This variety is often said to be to Germany what the Chardonnay is to France. Like Chardonnay, Riesling is one of the "noble" varieties, and as such its popularity has led to plantings throughout the world. Riesling, by nature, carries a fairly high acidity, particularly in cool climates. This makes an excellent counterweight for varying degrees of residual sugar in the wines. This natural acid backbone allows Rieslings, whether made sweet or dry, to age gracefully and improve and develop over time.

HARVEST	– late-ripening: mid to late October
SOILS	– preference for well drained, poor fertility.
CLIMATE	– cool climates preferred
YIELDS	– variable: (60–80 hl/ha average)

Pinot Blanc is the original French name of this variety which is thought to be a mutation of the Pinot Gris, which is a direct mutation of the Pinot Noir - the famous red variety from Burgundy. The wine does not have a specific varietal bouquet, its aroma is shy but remembered often as lindentree flowers. It is an elegant, harmonious and full-mouthed wine with good extract sensation but without feeling heavy and filling. Wines from ripe grapes often have a taste of "fresh bread". A perfect companion for Pacific salmon.

HARVEST	– early ripening: mid to late September
SOILS	– deep and/or stony soils
CLIMATE	– cool climates preferred
YIELDS	– moderate: (60–80 hl/ha)

Varietal: A varietal wine is any wine that is distinguished by and labelled according to the grape variety from which it was made. For example, Chardonnay wine is made from the Chardonnay grape.
* **Hl/ha** is the common measure of yield and refers to amount of juice measured in hundreds of litres (hecto-litres) per hectare of vineyard, for example, 40 hl/ha = 4000 litres from 1 hectare vineyard.

Red

CABERNET FRANC
(Cab'-air'nay Fronc)

Cabernet Franc is perhaps most famous for its contribution to the truly great wines of Saint-Emilion, Bordeaux. It is also the sole constituent of most of the finest red wines of the Loire Valley in France.

HARVEST – late-ripening: mid to late October
SOILS – clays (can withstand some wetness)
CLIMATE – moderate, requires fairly long season to ripen fully
YIELDS – moderate: (55–65 hl/ha)

PINOT NOIR
(Pee-no Nwahr)

Responsible for all the great red wines of Burgundy and one of the main varieties in French Champagne, this old, traditional, yet temperamental grape has long been admired for its superlative quality. Pinot Noir produces wines of much more finesse in regions of moderate heat, and particularly in areas where the late-season nights tend to be quite cool. There is a very pronounced relationship between the yield of Pinot Noir and the quality of the fruit produced.

HARVEST – mid-season ripening: early October
SOILS – well drained, calcareous soils
CLIMATE – cool climates preferred
YIELDS – very low: (25–40 hl/ha)

CABERNET SAUVIGNON
(Cab'-air-nay So'-vin-yawn)

The red grape of Bordeaux, and in particular, of the Medoc and Graves, Cabernet Sauvignon's popularity has taken it far from its native Bordeaux to the vineyards of both North and South America, Australia, New Zealand and South Africa. Due in part to the thick skins of the berries and the high pulp to pip ratio, the wines from this grape can be "massive," very deeply coloured and extremely tannic, particularly in warm climates. These characteristics give the wine a natural affinity for oak aging, and as a result are long-lived, sturdy and greatly improved with age.

HARVEST – late-ripening: mid to late October
SOILS – less fertile, well drained
CLIMATE – warm, long growing season
YIELDS – low: (35–50 hl/ha)

MERLOT
(Mair-lo)

The third variety of the classic Bordeaux trio of noble grapes, the Merlot currently occupies more hectares of Bordeaux vineyard than both Cabernets together. Although it is the sole constituent of such fine wines as the classified growths of Saint-Emilion and Pomerol, it is most often blended with the Cabernets to add a softening touch to the wine. Merlot wine is naturally supple and velvety smooth due to its soft tannins and relatively low acidity.

HARVEST – mid-season: early to mid October
SOILS – clays
CLIMATE – moderate, not too wet during ripening
YIELDS – generous: (70–80 hl/ha with quality)

HARVESTING

CROSS-SECTION OF A RIESLING GRAPE

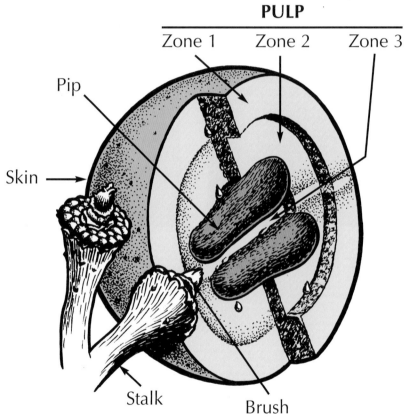

PULP

Zone 1   Zone 2   Zone 3

Pip

Skin →

Stalk

Brush

Zone 2 releases its juice first. **Zone 1** is in contact with the skin and **Zone 3** with the pips, thus requiring gentle pressure for complete juice extraction.

When the grapes are harvested from the vineyard and delivered to the winery, they are inspected for maturity, ripeness (sugar content, acid and pH) and soundness to determine the beginning of the winemaking process.

The ripeness or sugar content of the grapes is ascertained by the winemaker's palate and is measured technically by the use of a refractometer (see illustration). The grape sugars are also monitored in the vineyard by taking samples with the refractometer during the ripening season.

Brix = Degrees Brix (also known as Balling) is a measurement used by winemakers to define the sweetness (relative maturity) of grapes. Degrees Brix refers to the percentage of dissolved solids in the juice (almost all of which are sugars) and can be used by the winemaker to calculate the natural potential alcohol of the wine to be made, as illustrated in the chart below. As a rule of thumb, the natural potential alcohol can be calculated by dividing Brix of the fruit at harvest by two.

The Refractometer

The reading in the refractometer (as illustrated right) indicates a **Brix** measurement of 21.5, which translates to 11.3% potential alcohol.

The chart below shows three systems for measuring the sugar content of grapes and their relationship to the potential alcohol of the resulting wine.

MEASUREMENTS OF SUGAR CONTENT

Specific Gravity	1.085	1.090	1.095	1.100	1.105
°Oechsle (Germany)	85	90	95	100	105
Baumé (France)	11.3	11.9	12.5	13.1	13.7
Brix (North America)	**20.4**	**21.5**	**22.5**	**23.7**	**24.8**
% Potential Alcohol	10.6	11.3	11.9	12.5	13.1

COOPERAGE The Art of Barrel Making

The use of oak in wine dates back over 2000 years.

Cooperage is the craft of making barrels and the craftsman is known as the cooper. The barrel making process for wine is an old and time-honoured one and is illustrated in its seven stages in the photographs on these pages.

The selection of wood used is as important to the cooper as the selection of grapes is to the winemaker. The winemaker can choose barrels made from many forests of oak. Many of the most prized are French (as illustrated below):

Limousin, Nevers, Troncais, Allier and Vosges. These different types of oak have varying degrees of porousness that range from "open grain" to "tight grain" (see page 40).

Winemakers also use American Oak which generally imparts more oak flavour, an almost "sweetish" taste used generally for heavier wines. European Oak contributes more extract and more tannin to wine and yet less flavour per unit of extract of phenolic compounds. Experienced tasters can often determine which oak was used in the aging of a particular wine.

THE OAK FORESTS OF FRANCE

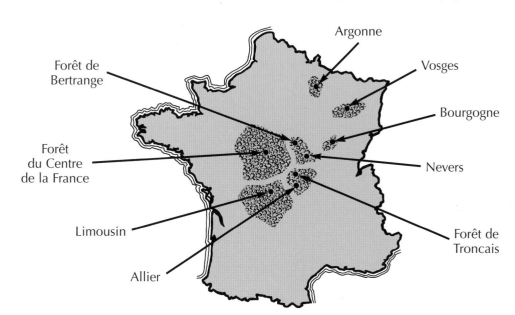

Argonne
Vosges
Bourgogne
Nevers
Forêt de Troncais
Forêt de Bertrange
Forêt du Centre de la France
Limousin
Allier

1. SPLITTING

2. DRYING

3. ASSEMBLING & SHAPING

4. FIRST FIRING

5. SECOND FIRING (toasting)

6. HEADS

7. FINISHING

HISTORY OF THE CORK

The use of natural cork as a closure for wine bottles is a centuries-old practice that continues today.

Cork is obtained from the layer just beneath the bark of the cork oak tree (Quercus suber), grown most extensively in Portugal (see photo, top left), Spain and Algeria, and to a lesser extent in other Mediterranean countries.

The cork oak tree has a life span of 300–400 years, although they seldom grow to heights of more than twelve metres. The trees must be approximately fifty years of age before they produce cork of a quality suitable for wine stoppers.

Once a tree is ready for harvest, workers strip the bark using long-handled hatchets (see photo, top right). This occurs during the months of June, July and August. Each individual tree may only be harvested once every eight to ten years.

Oblong sections of bark are carefully pried off the tree using the wedge-shaped handle of the hatchet. The inner layer of cork bark (the peridium) will continue to produce cork as long as it has not been bruised by the stripper's hatchet.

Slabs of stripped bark are then boiled and the tough, gritty outer layer is scraped off. The boiling dissolves tannic acid from the cork and softens the material so that the slabs can be straightened out, laid flat and packed into bundles.

The cork bottle closures are punched out of these slabs (see photo, right), sorted for quality, sterilized and packaged for shipment worldwide. At Inniskillin we use only the highest-grade quality corks for our wines.

DE-STEMMING/CRUSHING

Having been harvested, the grapes are delivered to the winery where they are immediately de-stemmed and crushed by means of a De-stemmer/Crusher. This process is quality driven since prolonged contact of the juice and the stems and leaves can impart undesirable bitterness to the resulting wine.

In the case of white winemaking from blue grapes, hand-harvested grapes are often pressed without being crushed. The pure crushed grapes (now called "must") are then pumped directly into the press.

Above: *Stainless steel auger*

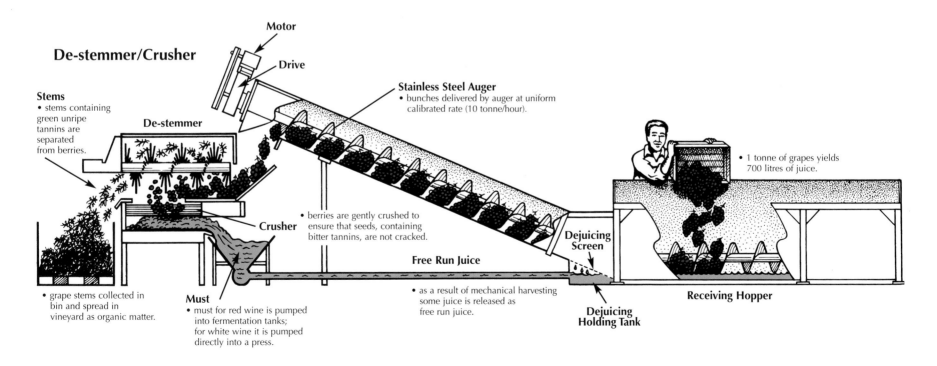

De-stemmer/Crusher

Motor

Drive

Stainless Steel Auger
• bunches delivered by auger at uniform calibrated rate (10 tonne/hour).

Stems
• stems containing green unripe tannins are separated from berries.

De-stemmer

• berries are gently crushed to ensure that seeds, containing bitter tannins, are not cracked.

Crusher

Free Run Juice

• 1 tonne of grapes yields 700 litres of juice.

Dejuicing Screen

• grape stems collected in bin and spread in vineyard as organic matter.

Must
• must for red wine is pumped into fermentation tanks; for white wine it is pumped directly into a press.

• as a result of mechanical harvesting some juice is released as free run juice.

Dejuicing Holding Tank

Receiving Hopper

29

PRESSING

The must goes directly into the grape press where the pure juice is then separated from the skins, pulp and seeds.

The Horizontal Pneumatic Press utilizes an inflatable bladder running the length of the press along a central shaft. When the press is loaded, the bladder is in a collapsed state, tightly covering the shaft. As the must falls into the press, the shaft slowly rotates, spreading it evenly inside the cage.

During this stage approximately 50 percent of the juice runs off through tiny perforations in the stainless steel cage of the press into a holding tank below. In principle, this press is identical to the traditional horizontal presses used throughout history. This pre-pressing run-off juice is referred to as "free run."

Once the press has been loaded to capacity, the cage is closed and then rotated for further de-juicing. The bladder can then be inflated inside the cage to press the grapes gently against the inside perforated wall of the cage.

The pressed de-juiced must, referred to at this stage as "pomace", is then unloaded from the press and can either be used for the distillation of brandy or spread in the vineyard as organic mulch.

The Wine Press and the Information Revolution

Over 500 years ago, while watching wine being made, Johann Gutenberg noticed the impression the wine press made in the must. He concluded that he could use the same principle to impress ink on paper – and thus the first printing press was born. Because of this monumental event, and thanks to the genius of Gutenberg and his love of wine, ideas and art have been reproduced and experienced by millions. So the next time you read a book, newspaper or magazine, make a toast to the art and power of wine.

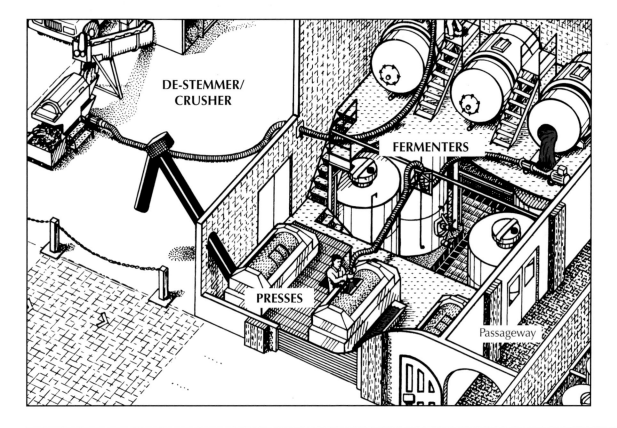

DE-STEMMER/CRUSHER

FERMENTERS

PRESSES

Passageway

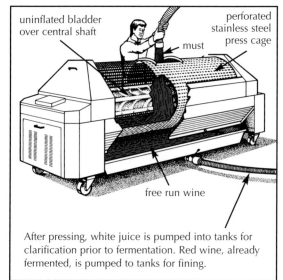

uninflated bladder over central shaft

perforated stainless steel press cage

must

free run wine

After pressing, white juice is pumped into tanks for clarification prior to fermentation. Red wine, already fermented, is pumped to tanks for fining.

CROSS-SECTION OF HORIZONTAL PNEUMATIC PRESS

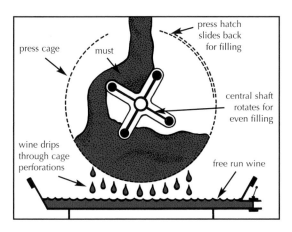

FILLING THE PRESS

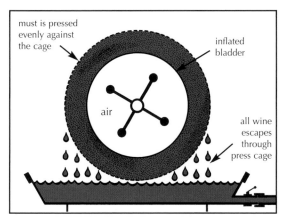

PRESSING THE MUST

Right: *Free run white juice draining from press **prior** to fermentation.*

Far right: *Free run red wine as it drains from press **after** fermentation*

FRESHLY PRESSED WHITE JUICE

FRESHLY PRESSED RED WINE

FERMENTATION

Colour & Tannin Extraction
(Red Wine varieties and Chardonnay)

Since all grape juice is white, the pigmentation from the skins is extracted in order to produce red wine.

To achieve this in an **Upright Fermenter,** the must (skins, pulp, seeds and juice) is circulated every four hours.

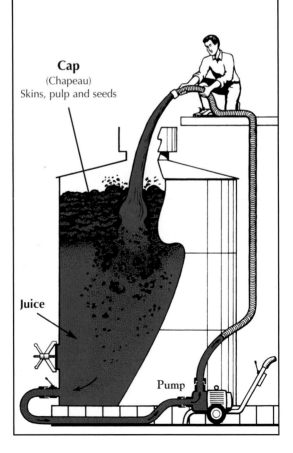

Cap
(Chapeau)
Skins, pulp and seeds

Juice

Pump

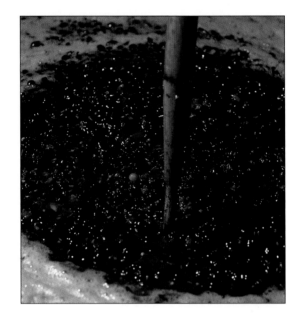

Primary Alcoholic Fermentation

This is the process whereby yeast metabolizes the natural grape sugars, thus producing alcohol and carbon dioxide (CO_2) as the two main by-products. Technically this is how grape juice turns into wine.

The process of fermentation also generates a tremendous amount of heat (another by-product), and must therefore be controlled by the

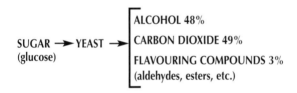

SUGAR → YEAST →
(glucose)

ALCOHOL 48%
CARBON DIOXIDE 49%
FLAVOURING COMPOUNDS 3%
(aldehydes, esters, etc.)

Cap

Fin

Roto-Fermenter

As illustrated at right, the cap is mixed with the juice by the rotation of the "fins" inside the tank.

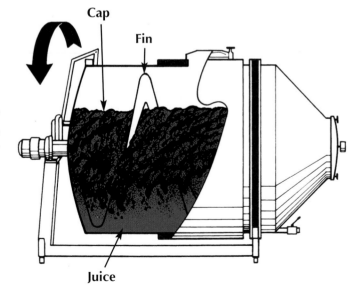

Juice

use of cooling jackets (bands of dimpled plates located on the outside of the tanks, circulating the cooling agent). The temperature of the fermentation is critical to the ultimate quality of the wine, especially white wine.

The rate of conversion of sugar to alcohol, being a natural process, is subject to many influences including temperature, yeast strain, yeast population, harvest variations and cellar conditions. As a result, fermentation can take as little as 24 hours to complete, or as long as one month or longer. A normal duration is approximately one week.

In a Roto-Fermenter, as illustrated on the opposite page, the "cap" (the name given to the skins, pulp and seeds) is mixed with the juice by the rotation of the fins inside the tank.

Malo-lactic Fermentation

Although not a true fermentation by technical definition, this is often referred to as a secondary fermentation. It is also referred to as "the flowering of the wine" because when it occurs in the spring, it coincides with the flowering of the vines or blossoming. Malo-lactic fermentation (M-L) is an organic process performed by naturally occurring bacteria that feed on the wine's natural malic acid, converting it to the softer lactic acid. This process effectively reduces the overall natural acidity of the wine, and in so doing adds a certain character and complexity to the wine.

M-L, as it is commonly called, is known to enhance red wines and is therefore common practice in red wine vinification. However, it is only selectively encouraged in white wines.

Chardonnay is the white wine variety most likely to benefit from M-L. Most other white wines of a more fruity character, and all naturally sweet wines, do not undergo an M-L fermentation.

Malic acid, derived from the Latin word malum or apple, indicates the sharp tartness of green apples. Lactic, derived from lactis, or milk, indicates the soft butteriness often used to describe Chardonnay. Malo-lactic fermentation is the process that transforms the one acid to the other and subsequently the one sensation to the other.

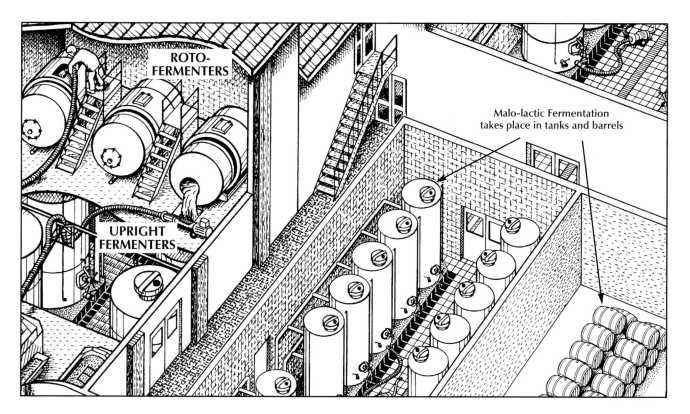

Malo-lactic Fermentation takes place in tanks and barrels

ROTO-FERMENTERS

UPRIGHT FERMENTERS

Above: *Releasing of CO_2 through fermentation (air) locks.*

RED WINES

After the red grapes are crushed and de-stemmed, the must is then pumped into a fermenting tank. It is inoculated with a pure strain yeast culture. The red must is fermented at temperatures between 25–30° C (much higher than the fermentation temperatures for white wine).

The colour of red wine is a result of the extraction of the colouring compounds from the grape skins, facilitated by the warmth created by the fermentation process. The carbon dioxide gas resulting from the fermentation causes the solid portion of the must to rise in the tank forming the cap. The extraction of colour takes place only in the area of contact between the cap and the juice, which is also the zone of highest temperature. Therefore, in order to get the maximum extraction, the juice must somehow contact all of the skins. This can be achieved by several means.

Remontage is a method of pumping the juice from under the cap back over the top of it to soak

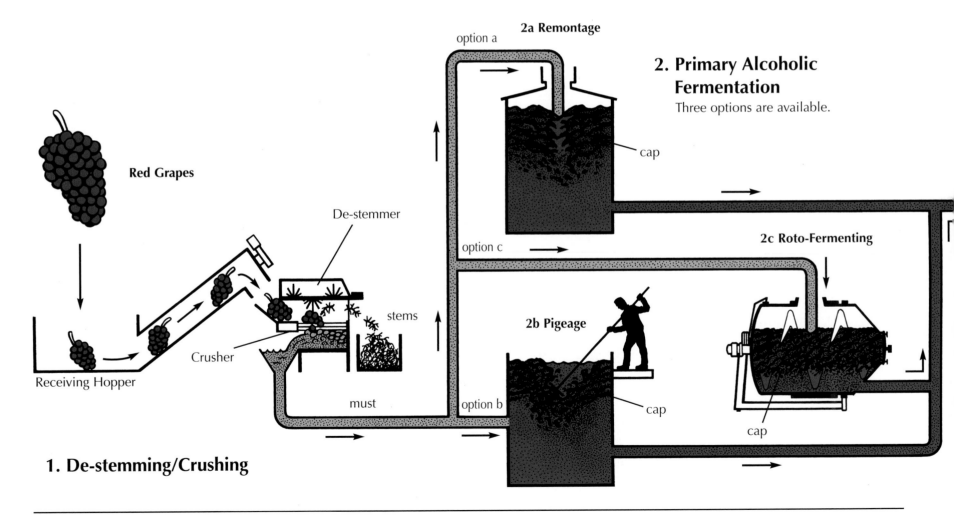

2a Remontage

option a

2. Primary Alcoholic Fermentation
Three options are available.

cap

2c Roto-Fermenting

option c

De-stemmer

stems

2b Pigeage

Red Grapes

Crusher

must

option b

cap

cap

Receiving Hopper

1. De-stemming/Crushing

34

the drier skins on top. It mixes the cooler and warmer juice, and aerates the wine (to help perpetuate fermentation). Another option is the traditional Burgundian method of pigeage, in which the floating cap is physically pushed under the liquid and mixed in with it. Although the most demanding technique, this is also one of the most efficient in terms of extraction. In a Roto-Fermenter, which replicates pigeage with technology, the cap is mixed in with the juice by the rotation of the tank itself. Fins inside the tank fold the cap over the juice. This is an efficient technique, particularly adapted to accommodate larger volumes of must.

It is through the physical contact between the underlying juice and the cap that red wine acquires the colour, tannins and flavours that give it its character. Upon completion of the primary alcoholic fermentation, the fermented must is then pressed and sent to oak barrels or tanks where it undergoes malo-lactic fermentation.

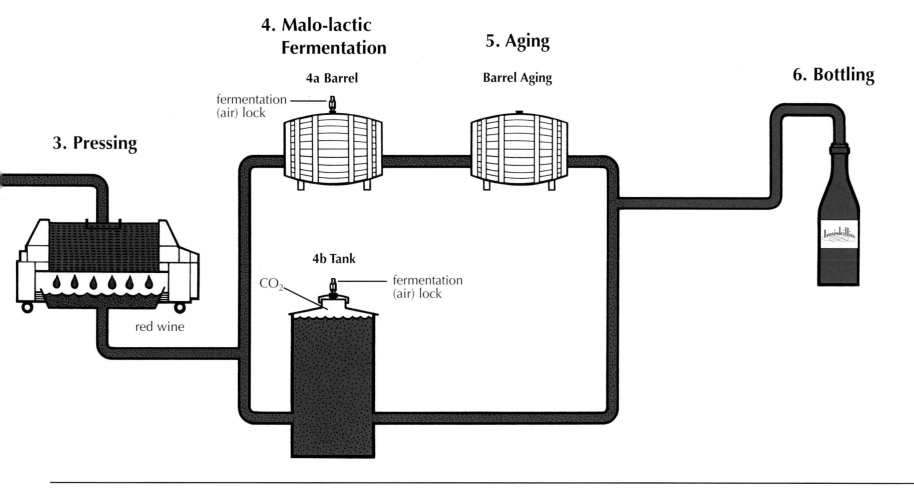

4. Malo-lactic Fermentation

4a Barrel

fermentation (air) lock

5. Aging

Barrel Aging

6. Bottling

3. Pressing

red wine

4b Tank

CO_2

fermentation (air) lock

Inniskillin

WHITE WINES

All white wine grapes, having been analyzed for quality, are de-stemmed and crushed en route to the press. The must is then pressed in order to separate the juice from the skins, pulp and seeds.

The juice is then cooled to between 8 and 12° C on its way to the tank cellar for settling. The juice rests peacefully in a tank for a period of about 48 hours. During this time it is naturally clarified by the set-

tling out of solids that are subsequently left behind in the tank by the "racking." Racking is the process of pumping the juice off the sediment to another tank. After racking, the clear juice is inoculated

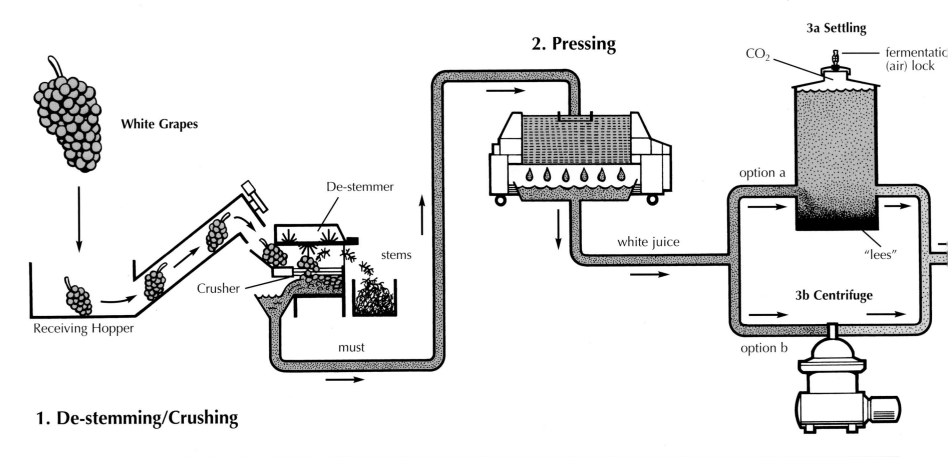

3. Juice Clarification
two options

3a Settling

CO_2

fermentatic (air) lock

option a

"lees"

white juice

3b Centrifuge

option b

2. Pressing

White Grapes

De-stemmer

stems

Crusher

Receiving Hopper

must

1. De-stemming/Crushing

with a pure strain yeast culture which is responsible for the primary fermentation that changes the grape juice into wine. Following the inoculation, the juice may ferment in a stainless steel tank or in oak barrels, depending on the winemaker's plan. Upon completion of the primary fermentation, the white wine is then racked into a stainless steel tank or into oak barrels for further aging.

4. Primary Alcoholic Fermentation (yeast added)

(Malo-lactic fermentation is an additional option for certain white wines)

5. Aging

6. Fining/Clarification

8. Bottling

4a Barrel

fermentation (air) lock

Barrel Aging

4b Tank

CO_2

fermentation (air) lock

7. Filtering

Inniskillin

TANK CELLAR

Settling/Clarification

Immediately following the pressing, the juice is cooled to 8–12° C in order to inhibit oxidation, yeast and enzyme activity, and to facilitate the settling of solids in the juice. The removal of these solids is an important step prior to fermentation, as they can be a source of bitterness, off-odours and off-flavours in the resulting wine.

Fining

Fining is a dual-purpose procedure in which a fining agent is added to the wine in order to remove small suspended particles. This will serve to clarify the wine. It also stabilizes the wine by removing substances such as yeast cells and proteins that could cause cloudiness, spoilage or precipitation later on. When the fining agent is added, tiny particles cling to it and then settle to the bottom of the tank. The wine can then be either racked or filtered off the sediment, thus removing the particles and the fining agent at the same time. Commonly used fining agents include: gelatin, egg whites

(see photo above), isinglass (a natural fish-derived protein) and bentonite (a type of refined clay).

Filtration

Filtration, normally the final step in the vinification of a wine, is the process of pumping a wine through a filter medium under pressure. Basically a process of absorption, filtration serves to remove suspended particles, clarifying the wine. It also further removes possible contaminants such as residual yeast or bacteria, thereby stabilizing the wine as well. Barrel-aged wines do not necessarily require filtration.

Above; *Egg whites being prepared for use as final fining agent.*

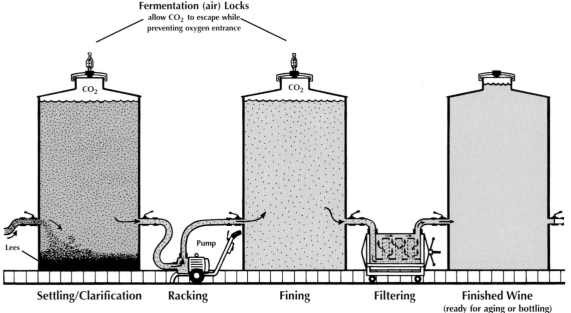

Fermentation (air) Locks
allow CO₂ to escape while preventing oxygen entrance

Lees

Pump

| Settling/Clarification | Racking | Fining | Filtering | Finished Wine |

Finished Wine
(ready for aging or bottling)

BARREL AGING

BARREL AGING The Influence of Oak in Wine

The cost is high, approximately $800 per 225 litre barrel. Expensive? Yes! But many of the world's finest wines owe their share of character, complexity and quality to aging in small oak barrels. There are numerous variables when choosing a wine barrel. Each wine style requires a different oak flavour. The winemaker has the opportunity to choose the cooper, wood type, forest, grain, size of barrel and the toast. The grain may be "open" or "tight", as can be seen in the illustrations below. There are choices of barrel shape – Bordeaux (tall and narrow) and Burgundian (short and broad). There is also a choice between thinner staved "Chateau" and the thicker staved "Export" barrels.

GRAIN	FOREST	CHARACTERISTICS
OPEN	LIMOUSIN	Limousin wood perfumes and colours the wine rapidly with little finesse.
AVERAGE	BOURGOGNE NEVERS	Bourgogne and Nevers wood gives a vanilla flavour and balance to the wine.
TIGHT	ALLIER TRONCAIS VOSGES	The wood of Allier, Troncais and Vosges releases its perfumes slowly, with finesse.

LIMOUSIN OAK - OPEN GRAIN

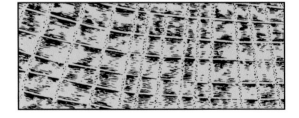

TRONCAIS OAK - TIGHT GRAIN

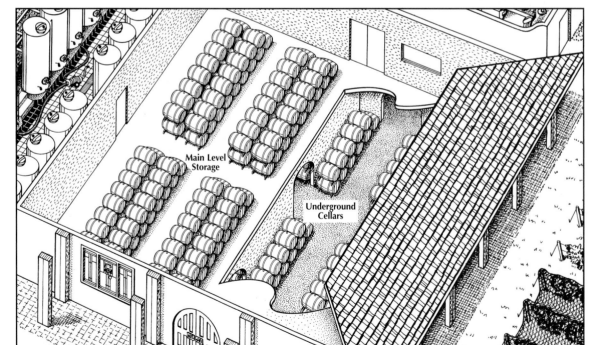

Main Level Storage

Underground Cellars

The changes that occur during the wine's aging process are enormously complex. In barrel aging there are two aging functions. The first is extraction in which the tannins, vanilla, oak lactones and other phenolics are extracted from the wood. The second is oxidation in which the tannins, acids and other components of the wine react to a gradual exposure to oxygen through the grain of the wood.

The amount and type of aging that a wine should receive are both a function of the wine qualities such as colour or tannin, and the style of wine that is being produced.

For the first three years, barrels are used particularly for their extractives, as the total extractables offered up by the wood decrease dramatically after this time. In the fourth, fifth and sixth years a barrel is used primarily as a *barrique d'occasion* for the express purpose of slow oxidation (as the wood breathes) with a negligible absorption of extracts.

Tartrate crystals which appear on the barrel are naturally occurring crystals often referred to as "wine diamonds." When the grapes begin fermentation, they contain potassium from the soil where they grew and tartaric acid, a natural fruit acid present in ripe grapes. Through the increase in alcohol during fermentation, the potassium and the bitartrate of the tartaric acid are combined to form potassium bitartrate in solution form. Upon cooling, the solution changes to crystalline form and precipitates out of the wine. On occasion these crystals adhere to the barrel and may also occasionally occur in the bottle, most noticeably on the cork.

The barrel cellar on the main level is for the storage of red wines while the underground cellar, because it is cooler, is for the white wines.

Above: *Barrel aging.*

Below: *The Inniskillin Wine Library adjacent to the underground barrel aging cellars.*

Opposite page: *The underground barrel aging cellars.*

BRAE BURN VINEYARD – Niagara

Inniskillin's vineyard is called The Brae Burn Estate. "Brae Burn" is of Gaelic origin and translates literally as "Hill Stream," referring to the Niagara Escarpment and the Niagara River.

Brae Burn Estate, on which the winery is situated, is located on the Niagara Parkway just five minutes south of the historic town of Niagara-on-the-Lake and just twenty minutes north of Niagara Falls. While touring along the Niagara River, Sir Winston Churchill once referred to the Niagara Parkway as "the prettiest Sunday afternoon drive in the world."

The vineyard's soils consist of clay-loam with glacial and alluvial deposits, ideally suited for the growing of Vitis vinifera varieties, such as Pinot Noir. In addition, the winery is surrounded by vineyards dedicated to the production of Icewine.

A research vineyard for irrigation and wetlands research is also located on the property.

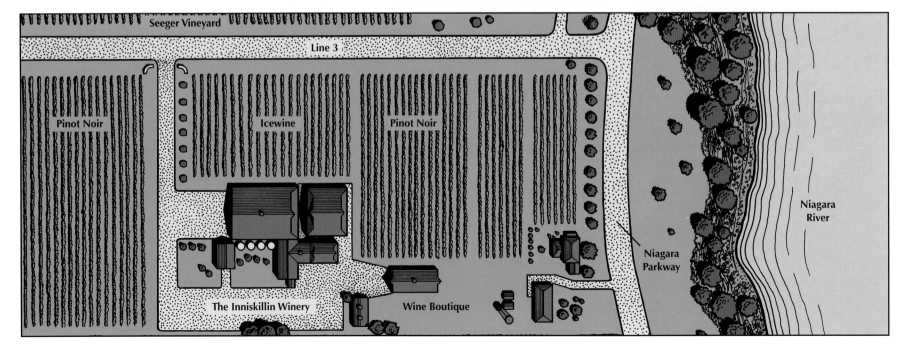

FRANK LLOYD WRIGHT

When we originally acquired the Brae Burn Estate, one of the original buildings was an old barn with a long, simple pitched roof and unusual overhanging peaks, and tongue and groove pine in the interiors. We discovered that this barn and two others on the Larkin Farm to the south were, in fact, "prairie barns," with ventilated overhangs pointed opposite to the prevailing winds to facilitate the drying of cereal grains and to protect them from blowing rain.

Research into the barns revealed an association between the Larkin building and Frank Lloyd Wright. Darwin D. Martin, the president of the Larkin Company of Buffalo, was one of Frank Lloyd Wright's greatest patrons. Over the years, there were nine major Wright commissions in the Buffalo/Niagara Frontier area (www.franklloydwright.com).

Frank Lloyd Wright revolutionized North American architecture. He rejected the classical designs borrowed from other worlds that so dominated the late nineteenth and early twentieth centuries. Instead he developed a form based on simplicity and the lessons of nature. He called it Organic Architecture.

Wright's bold marriage of natural form with modern creation is reflected in the Inniskillin philosophy of innovation inspired by tradition.

It was his intent "to make the building belong to the ground," and at Inniskillin we have always designed the structures of our estate winery with this spirit in mind.

Not so much bound by tradition as inspired by it.

Opposite page top: *View of Inniskillin from corner of Niagara Parkway and Line 3, with Niagara Escarpment in the background*

Bottom left: *Front entrance of the Wine Boutique in Brae Burn Barn.*

Below: *Front entrance to the Barrel Aging Cellar.*

PACIFIC NORTHWEST

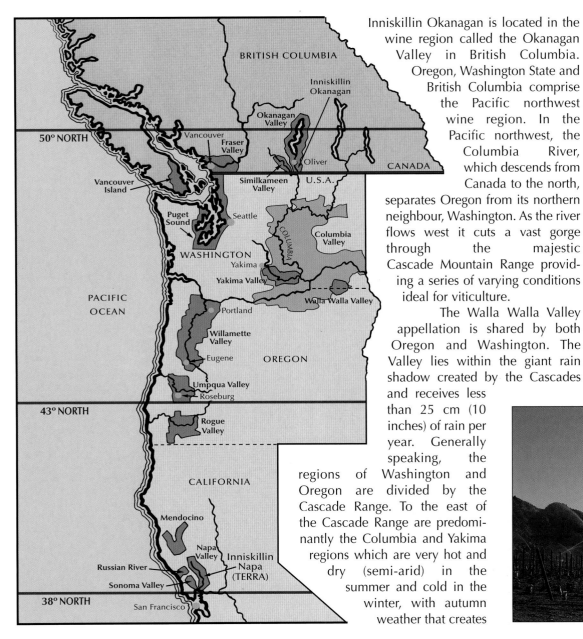

Inniskillin Okanagan is located in the wine region called the Okanagan Valley in British Columbia. Oregon, Washington State and British Columbia comprise the Pacific northwest wine region. In the Pacific northwest, the Columbia River, which descends from Canada to the north, separates Oregon from its northern neighbour, Washington. As the river flows west it cuts a vast gorge through the majestic Cascade Mountain Range providing a series of varying conditions ideal for viticulture.

The Walla Walla Valley appellation is shared by both Oregon and Washington. The Valley lies within the giant rain shadow created by the Cascades and receives less than 25 cm (10 inches) of rain per year. Generally speaking, the regions of Washington and Oregon are divided by the Cascade Range. To the east of the Cascade Range are predominantly the Columbia and Yakima regions which are very hot and dry (semi-arid) in the summer and cold in the winter, with autumn weather that creates wide temperature differences from day to night. Much of the area is semi-arid desert as is the Okanagan Valley, subsequently requiring irrigation. To the west, which is predominantly in Oregon (Willamette Valley) the weather is maritime, with dry, cool summers and wet, mild winters, located at approximately 45° latitude. The Coastal Mountains block out some of the ocean air and the rains come in September and early October similar to Niagara, Canada and Burgundy, France.

Washington has four appellation areas: Columbia Valley, Yakima Valley, Walla Walla Valley and Puget Sound (as illustrated in map) while Oregon has five appellation areas: Willamette, Walla Walla, Rogue River, Umpqua and Columbia River.

INNISKILLIN OKANAGAN

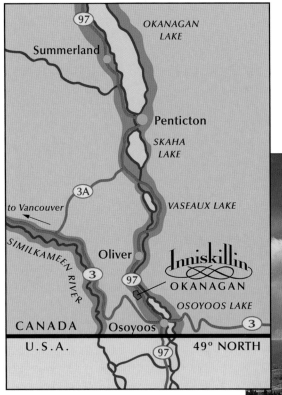

reflected the Native heritage. The label inspired the naming of our estate vineyard: Dark Horse Vineyard. You will also notice, in the photograph on page 48, the famous McIntyre Bluff known as the Chief, which is famous in Indian legend.

The Okanagan Valley climatic region is much dryer than Niagara and unique as a grape-growing region in western Canada. The valley is at the same latitude as the Rhine Valley in Germany and the Champagne region of France. The region stretches for 130 km, from Lake Osoyoos, on the 49° north latitude, just north of the Canada/US border, to the northern tip of Okanagan Lake. The lakes moderate the

Below: *Dark Horse Vineyard*

Inniskillin Okanagan commenced as a partnership between Inniskillin and the Inkameep Indian Band (Okanaquen Tribe) in the Okanagan Valley in British Columbia. Inniskillin established an estate winery in the Okanagan in 1994 which commemorated 20 years of Inniskillin's first crush.

The labels were designed by a local artist (see page 19). Great care was taken to ensure that the labels temperatures throughout the year. Intense sunlight and minimal rainfall allow the grapes to ripen to their full maturity, while cool nights help them to retain high acidity. These climatic conditions, along with a unique soil structure, produce wines that are full-bodied and highly flavoured with good acidity.

The climate is only one element of the larger system at play—called an ecosystem. The southern Okanagan Valley is positioned at the northernmost tip of the Sonoran Desert, starting in Mexico and extending through North America as the Great Basin, with ancient origins probably dating back 10,000 years. The Valley provides the hot, dry summers and mild winters characteristic of the arid antelope-brush ecosystem. In the warmest part of the south Okanagan Valley is a pocket of dry grassland dominated by bunchgrasses, the wind, and the scraggly dark branches of antelope-brush.

This region is home to a diverse array of uniquely adapted wildlife species such as the Burrowing Owl, Northern Rattlesnake, Tiger Salamander and Wind Scorpion, to name a few.

This region is ideally suited for the growing of premium vinifera grapes. Annual precipitation is about 25 cm. Moisture from precipitation travels quickly through the sandy or gravelly soils, so few plants can grow in these soils in arid areas. The low available water storage capacity of the soils therefore requires irrigation in order to grow grapevines in these otherwise desert conditions.

On the east side of the Okanagan Valley are moderately sloping terraces and benches (Osoyoos Lake Bench) that lie between the northeast side of Osoyoos Lake and the steep, rocky mountain slopes to the east. Inkameep and Mica Creeks, passing westward through the area, provide the main drainage. The soil of this area is derived from windblown sands and gravels deposited by the meltwaters of the Ice Age glaciers.

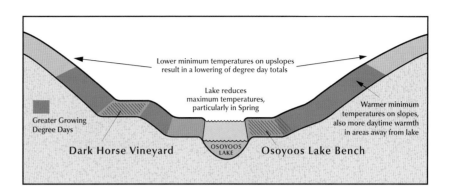

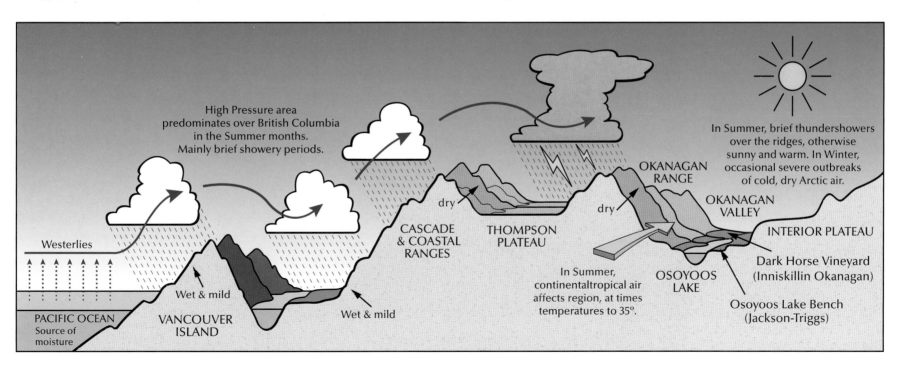

The surficial geologic materials (soil parent materials) are dominantly sandy glaciofluvial deposits, some with gravelly subsoils. Very fine sandy and coarse silty glaciolacustrine deposits also occur in the vicinity of Inkameep Creek and probably underlie portions of the sandy glaciofluvial materials at depth elsewhere. Thin, sandy veneers of eolian (windblown) material sometimes occurs in areas protected from the wind. Along the extreme eastern boundary of the area, large boulders and stones sometimes occur on, and in, the soil. These originated from the adjacent steep, rocky mountain slopes. The soils are all Brown Chernozems (as classified in the Canadian Soil Classification). They have a grayish brown surface horizon about 15 cm thick that is slightly enriched with organic matter. Under this is moderately weathered yellowish brown to light brown zone that is about 20 cm thick and usually non-calcareous. Under this is unweathered soil parent material that is sometimes calcareous.

On the west side of the Valley, the soils underlying the Inniskillin Dark Horse Vineyard are classified as Ratnip (soil parental materials), which consist of gravelly, coarse textured fluvial fan deposits. Textures range from gravelly, sandy loam to gravelly loamy sand. Surface stones vary from few on the fan apron to many at the fan apex — much of it from the Hester Creek Fan deposits.

Top right: *Ancient pictograph on wall inside of cave overlooking Inkameep Vineyard.*

Below: *Inkameep Vineyard and McIntyre Bluff in the background to the left.*

ICEWINE

Originally developed in the cool climate wine regions of Europe — Germany and Austria — the production of Icewine is ideally suited to Niagara's climatic conditions.

The grapes are left on the vine well into December and January. The ripe berries are dehydrated through the constant freezing and thawing during these winter conditions. This remarkable process concentrates the sugars, acids and extracts in the berries thereby intensifying the flavours and giving Icewine its immense complexity.

The entire vineyard is carefully covered with netting to protect the sweet ripe berries from ravaging birds. Some of the crop is lost to wind damage.

The grapes are painstakingly picked by hand in their naturally frozen state, ideally at temperatures of -10 to -13° C, sometimes forcing us to pick in the middle of the night. Yields are very low, often as little as 5–10 percent of a normal yield. The frozen grapes are pressed in the extreme cold. Much of the water in the juice remains frozen as ice crystals during the pressing and only a few drops of sweet concentrated juice are salvaged. The juice is then fermented very slowly for several months and stops naturally at approximately 10–12 percent alcohol.

Icewine tastes intensely sweet and flavourful in the initial mouth sensation. The balance is achieved by the acidity which creates a clean, dry finish to the taste. The nose is reminiscent of lychee nuts and the wine tastes of tropical fruits with overtones of peach nectar and mango.

Historically, Icewine was first made in Germany in the mid-1700s. The quality of Icewine is primarily determined by how low the temperature drops at the time of harvest, resulting in high extract, fullness

Left: *Icewine grapes "naturally frozen on the vine," prior to hand harvesting.*

Right: *Grand Prix d'Honneur Award from Vinexpo, Bordeaux, France.*

and concentration of aroma in the final product.

The water in the berry is frozen and forms ice crystals which separate from the sugars, acids and flavour components. Once pressed, the ice crystals begin to melt, and therefore it is critical to monitor the Brix level of the juice being extracted to ensure the highest quality.

Icewines exhibit fresh, crisp, resonant flavours and aromas with a highly intense backbone of acidity which cleanses the palate and gives the wine depth, longevity and a long almost "peacock" aftertaste.

Another major characteristic of Icewine is its naturally high acidity, a direct function of cool climate viticulture regions. It is this acidity which distinguishes Icewine from most other dessert wines, and when in ideal equilibrium with the intensity of sugar created by the natural freezing process, is what makes Icewine such a unique and truly great wine.

German law reclassified Icewine in 1983, establishing -7 degrees Celsius as minimum temperature, and a must weight of 125 degrees Oechsle.

Below: *Harvesting Icewine grapes at night, December 22, at Brae Burn Estate.*

Top left: *Wild Berry Strudel with Yukon Jack Sabayon and fresh Niagara fruit basket, a perfect compliment to Icewine.*

The other important aspect of making Icewine is the pressing off of only the sweetest juice while the grapes are still naturally frozen (first pressing) and the termination of pressing as the juice starts to become diluted. The dilution is created by heat generated by the friction from the pressing which melts the frozen grapes.

An interesting paradox of a great Icewine is that it can be consumed shortly after bottling, at which time great freshness is maintained, or it can be aged for well over 20 years.

Icewine made from grapes "naturally frozen on the vine" are markedly different, with more mineral enrichment and distinctive and intense aromas.

When Icewines are in their youth, they are fresh and clean on the finish, whereas older Icewines tend to be heavy and stronger in flavour, and linger on the palate longer.

Canada is blessed with cold winters. Yet weather is always a factor, as in 1997, when a mild winter brought on by the El Niño weather pattern almost ruined the prospects for Icewine in Canada.

Due to the warm growing seasons, as illustrated in chart B, page 15, the grapes grown in Canada frequently mature with high grape sugars. Temperatures of -11 degrees Celsius results on average at 42 degrees Brix at harvest.

Right: *Icewine grapes "naturally frozen on the vine," on the Dark Horse Estate Vineyard, in the Okanagan Valley.*

HARVEST:
December to January

HARVEST TEMPERATURES:
-10° C to -13° C

PICKING:
Hand harvested (exclusively), naturally frozen on the vine, normally throughout the night (coldest part of the day).

YIELD:
Extremely low (approx. 5%–10% of a normal harvest)

FOOD AND WINE

In our search for culinary excellence, we Canadians have discovered that distinctiveness and diversity exist here at home. Regional foods have joined with locally produced wines to form an identifiable, original Canadian culinary style, one that reflects the land, the people and the foods we produce.

Canadian chefs head into the country to stock their kitchens with locally grown fruits and vegetables. The Aboriginal people planted beans, squash and corn, foods now celebrated in Canadian cuisine. In Quebec, cheese varieties like Oka and Ermite Blue cheese were developed over a century ago by local monks. Ontario's chefs are incorporating fiddleheads (pictured to the right) with maple syrup, and traditional game animals are being farmed, bringing venison and other delicacies back to the gourmet table. British Columbia's famed salmon (see next page) forms the base of many brilliant new dishes.

Canadian wine, being cool climate wine, always retains a pleasant backbone of acidity, which clears the palate between bites. This makes Canadian wine an ideal partner to a wide variety of dishes.

In *The Food and Wine Adventure Series*, our resident chef, Isabela Kalabis, has married an array of Canadian foods to our line of varietal wines. The textures, aromas and flavours of the food mix

with the body, aromas and flavours of the wines to create a truly unique Canadian gastronomic experience.

Let us not forget the simple pleasures of wine and food and their relevance to our daily lives.

More pleasure for your nose, more zest for your palate!

To fully appreciate the personality of different grape varieties and the subtle character of wine, it is essential to have an appropriately fine-tuned glass shape. The shape is responsible for the flow of the wine and consequently where it touches the various taste zones of the tongue. The initial point of contact depends on the shape and volume of the glass, the diameter of the rim and its finish. Once the tongue is in

contact with the wine, three messages are transmitted at the same time: temperature, texture and taste. Wine is composed of different elements: fruit, acidity, mineral components, tannin and alcohol. The combination between the sense of smell and taste leads into the wonderful world of flavour. It is the glass shape which is responsible for balance and harmony of flavours. Riedel was the first to discover the concept: "The content commands the shape!"

On October 18, 1999, Riedel and Inniskillin conducted an Icewine workshop to create the ultimate Icewine glass. From the prototype developed at the workshop, an exquisite vessel emerged from which is delivered the ultimate experience of Icewine for your palate.

Right: *A sketch of the Icewine glass prototype by George Riedel.*
Above: *The Inniskillin Wine Library adjacent to the underground barrel aging cellars.*
Left: *Wild B.C. Salmon Tartare and Gravlax with Dilled Crème Fraîche and Caviar.*
Opposite page left: *Inniskillin Founders' Reserve 1997 Pinot Noir.*
Opposite page right: *Fiddlehead and Scallop Salad with Cranberry Dressing.*

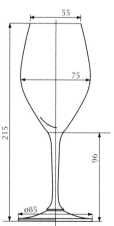

HEALTH

Wine has always played an integral part in the health and happiness of mankind.

On Sunday, November 5, 1998, CBC's *60 Minutes* gave a phenomenal boost to the wine industry. They revealed scientific evidence that moderate wine consumption with meals helps to prevent heart disease. Morley Safer interviewed two scientists who found that despite similar fat intake, France's heart attack rate was one-third that of the US. A key attributing factor is the French custom of drinking wine with meals. Antioxidants, in addition to alcohol, are likely to be responsible for wine's beneficial effects.

Commonly referred to as the "French Paradox" first aired on *60 Minutes*, the phenolic compound resveratrol is considered one of the agents in wine which causes a decrease in cardiovascular disease and possibly certain cancers.

Phenols and polyphenols are complex substances found primarily in grape skins that give wine their characteristic aroma, flavours and mouth feel. Because red wines tend to have longer skin contact during fermentation, they are higher than whites in phenolic compounds, including resveratrol. Resveratrol was used in ancient Japanese and Chinese folk remedies and was believed to reduce "bad" cholesterol and prevent blood clotting.

Resveratrol is a natural fungicide in the skin of grapes. It provides protection for the grape in cool, damp climates. The more cool and humid the climate, the more resveratrol is produced naturally to combat mildew, an interesting phenomena of cool climate viticulture. Grapes grown in hot, dry climates such as California, Italy and Australia do not require protection and so do not contain high levels of the flavanoid. Pinot Noir is the exception, as high levels of resveratrol are found in this grape wherever it is grown. Wines from Niagara, Burgundy, Oregon and New York have the highest levels, according to Dr. David Goldberg, Professor of Biochemistry, University of Toronto.

Left: *Riedel glass, on Canadian burled maple table, with reflection of FLW.*

CCOVI – Cool Climate Oenology & Viticulture Institute

The Cool Climate Oenology and Viticulture Institute, known as CCOVI, is on the Brock University campus in Niagara, Canada. The CCOVI building was named Inniskillin Hall to honour Inniskillin Wines. This state-of-the-art teaching and research facility was officially opened on June 11, 1999. Inniskillin Hall will also house a pilot winery, professional tasting lab for wine evaluation, a Canadian Wine Library and the Enoteca for international wines.

The mission of CCOVI is to meet the research and education needs of the cool climate growing and wine producing regions of the world. Its roles are to pursue the groundbreaking research and leading technologies necessary to maintain and enhance the competitive position of Canada's grape growers, vintners and related professionals and to foster partnerships and collaborative efforts between these groups and the worldwide academic community. The Institute also provides education programs granting degrees in Oenology and Viticulture (the first students enrolled in 1997).

CCOVI has incorporated biotechnology labs in order to focus on biotechnology research into the next millennium. It will have great potential in taking the best features from clonal selection, plant breeding, genetics and other disciplines. Genetic engineering, as a positive tool in the natural control of diseases, offers many possibilities. We are all very concerned about the use of pesticides and this may dramatically reduce the use of chemicals of any kind. The advantages of this type of an approach are numerous and the perfection of the science of biotechnology will undoubtedly preoccupy scientists in viticultural research and oenology well into the next millennium.

The Institute's research programs will focus on the special needs of cool climate. It will work with Niagara College (Joint Research and Demonstration Vineyard), Okanagan University College (in British Columbia's Okanagan Valley), University of Guelph and numerous other institutions internationally. Karl Kaiser graduated from Brock University with a degree in Chemistry. Karl and myself were granted Honorary Degrees in Law, LLD, from Brock University.

"Every great viticulture and winemaking region in the world is associated with an institution of higher learning ... as is now the case with Canada."

– Dr. Donald Ziraldo

THE AUTHOR

Born in St. Catharines, Ontario, Donald J.P. Ziraldo is co-founder and President of Inniskillin Wines in Niagara-on-the-Lake, Canada.

After receiving his Bachelor of Science Degree in Agriculture from the University of Guelph in 1971, Ziraldo joined forces with Karl J. Kaiser to found Inniskillin Wines in 1975.

Challenged by the need to compete on the world stage, Ziraldo pioneered the estate winery movement in Canada. As part of his ongoing efforts to promote quality wines produced in Canada, Donald has been credited with founding the Vintners Quality Alliance (VQA), an organization responsible for maintaining the highest standards in viticulture and winemaking. Ziraldo is Founding Chairman of the VQA.

Inniskillin's commitment to the Ontario wine industry has resulted in many gold medals from international wine competitions. In 1991 Inniskillin competed against 4100 wines from across the world in Vinexpo in Bordeaux, France, and captured the Citadelle d'Or Award (Grand Prix d'Honneur), the highest award, given for its 1989 Icewine.

While he continues to raise awareness of the quality of Canadian wines, Ziraldo is also driven by a desire to globalize. In the early 1990s he established Inniskillin Napa Vineyards (Terra) in California's Napa Valley producing limited quantities of Merlot and Chardonnay (from the Sangiacomo Vineyard).

In 1993 Inniskillin formed a partnership with Jaffelin of Burgundy, France, to produce wines from Pinot Noir and Chardonnay grapes grown in Niagara, which were labelled under the name "ALLIANCE." This alliance evolved into Clos Jordan. In 1994 Inniskillin established

"Inniskillin Okanagan" in the Okanagan Valley in British Columbia.

Ziraldo's leadership has earned him numerous awards from the business and wine communities. In 1993 he was appointed to the Order of Ontario, which honours service of the greatest distinction of singular excellence which benefits society in Ontario and elsewhere. Other awards include Marketer of the Year by the American Marketing Association.

In 1994 he was granted an honorary Doctorate of Laws (LLD) from Brock University in Canada. In 1998, Donald was awarded the Order of Canada — the country's highest honour for lifetime achievement.

In November 1999, Donald was acknowledged as one of Canada's Top 25 CEOs of the Century by the *National Post* magazine.

Ziraldo's passions lie in skiing/snowboarding and his Art Deco collection which graces his home on the Niagara River Parkway in Niagara-on-the-Lake.